Poetry with a Vengeance

It is no loss to mankind when one writer decides to call it a day. When a tree falls in the forest, who cares but the monkeys?

—Richard Ford

Poetry with a Vengeance

Russell Bittner

Kelsay Books

© 2014 Russell Bittner . All rights reserved. This material may not be reproduced in any form, published, reprinted, recorded, performed, broadcast, rewritten or redistributed without explicit permission of Russell Bittner. All such actions are strictly prohibited by law.

ISBN 13: 978-0615958019

Cover Art: Margitay Tihamér (1859 -1922)

Kelsay Books
White Violet Press
24600 Mountain Avenue, 35
Hemet, California 92544

Contents

Pomelettes for Snarky Children

What Warmth Is There in One Old Tree?	11
This Rain That Wears No Raincoat	13
Four(teen)-letter Words	14
Habeas Corpus	15
Hurly-Burly	16
I Often Think I'd Like To Be	17
I Wonder, Shall I Ever See…	18
If Birds Could Swim	19
If Only I Could Be a Slug	21
Little Miss Muffet	22
Nolens Volens	24
The Butcher, the Baker, the Candlestick Maker	26
Time Runs the Boldest of Races	27
"Who Do Dat Voodoo?"	28
Ubiquitous Brown Birds	29

Potpourri or Pot pourri

A Letter to My Mother	33
ПИСЬМО К МАТЕРИ	35
9/11/03	37
A Body May With Wit Rebel	39
A Poet Writes in Silence	40
An Acorn's Got a Heritage	41
Any Dope Can Write a Ditty	42
Blizzard	43
Busted!	44
'Caned and Disabled	45
Coitus	47
Diminished Expectations	49
Epilogue to a *Splendid* Love Affair	51

Family Planning	52
Flight 103 to Lockerbie: Happy Anniversary!	53
From Dust We Come, to Dust We Go	54
I Like the Haze of Summer Days	55
I Like the Orange, but *Love* the Black	56
I Miss Her Most in Winter	57
I Prowl About My Garden	58
I Remember When I Was a Player	59
I Rummage 'Round in My Safe Place	60
I Watch a Spider Spin Her Web	61
I Wonder, Does a Tree Look Down?	62
I've Swooned to Sweet, Yet Scented Sour	63
If Love is to Cartography What Romance Is to Maps	64
In re: End of Days	65
It's Time To Do the Christmas Cards	66
Love Becomes You in the Fall	67
Love in Winter Storage	69
MAD* Mongers	70
March Snow	72
My Pears, My Port and My Stilton	73
Narcissus Meets Echo at the Weeping Well	74
Not Enough	75
Now, Where Would the First Wind Begin?	77
Out of a Rock, *NOW!*	78
Roulette	79
SAD Saps	80
"Screwered"	82
So, *This* Is How Old Forests Feel	83
Spell Unbounded	84
Stratifying the Stress	85
Surrender	86
The Ethos of Capital-isthmus	88
The Garden Lusts for Thrill Tonight	89
The Last Rose of Summer	90
The Moon Is Just a Calculus	91
The *Real* Object of Her Affection	92

"The Weather is for Kids, You Know"	94
There Are No Larks on Broadway	95
There's Nothing Left but Cigarettes	96
They Say that 'Orange' Has No Pair	97
Uneasy Traders	98
Waving Off the Last of Winter	99
What Moon Are You!	100
While Munching, I Muse on a Mural	101
Eldorado	102
Aubade to Marit – Never Sung	105

A Year of Musing Dangerously

January	111
February	112
March	114
April	116
May	117
June	118
July	119
August	120
September	121
October	122
November	123
December	124

Lite Verse

A Low I. Q. Haiku	127
A Poet and a Gardener	128
But Mondays-through-Fridays Are Hellishly Long!	129
Caveat poeta: lectores mordent	130
Cold	131
Girl from Baku	132
I Wish I Might've Found the Road to Oxbridge	134
It's 3 a.m., the Silent Hour	135

June bug	136
Little Gets Riddled	137
Spring Bling – Ka-*ching!*	138

Acknowledgments
About the Author

Pomelettes

for Snarky Children

What Warmth Is There in One Old Tree?

What warmth is there in one old tree
   with room enough for me and thee
to crawl inside and order tea
   and scones this red-nosed Monday?

Much more, I'd bet, than on the ground
   where snow and ice and dog— abound,
and boomers, in surround-sound, box
   our ears into next Tuesday.

If not a tree, let's find a lake
   and swap our tea and scones for cake,
then ratchet up the flame to bake
   our "catch" on pie-skied Wednesday.

If not a lake, at least a pond
   of which your forebears once were fond
before they slithered out to bond –
   less gills – one murky Thursday.

(A pond is but a toad's brass ring –
   theatrically, his chance to sing
as well *we* might before we bring
   the curtain down on Friday.)

But if you'd rather hug the bank
   because the last time out you sank
up to your knees in mud that stank
   of fish we caught on Saturday,

then let's just light a little fire
   and make of toads and fish a pyre,
and to our tree once more retire
   to sleep till Easter Sunday!

This Rain That Wears No Raincoat

This rain that wears no raincoat
   and has no claim on me
would just as soon I were the moon
   now floating out to sea.

This rain that scorns galoshes
   and rails at *bonhomie*
would suffer ill repute to boot
   a hooligan like me.

This rain that thinks umbrellas
   and plastic hats are twee
would find it hardly suitable
   that you now shelter me.

This rain that falls in buckets,
   then sets those buckets free
to sail away, extempore,
   means not a whit to me.

This rain that washes windows
   and falls by clouds' decree,
then reaches for a rainbow's hand
   has *nothing* over me.

Four(teen)-letter Words

Many are the words I know,
   but there's one I'm loath to use;
warily, I've watched it grow
   well beyond its terrible twos.

No, it's not the word I choose
   if, in saying it, I blush
euphemistically for "lose"
   what I urgently must flush.

Nor is it the one I slice
   when my brother makes me sick;
we say 'Richard' when he's nice;
   when he's not, he's one real 'Rick.'

True again for my big sis'
   when she's got an angry itch –
hang-nail, zit or sloppy kiss,
   she becomes a brazen … witch.

If I've caught you by surprise,
   wondering what it might be,
piqued as punch and yet not wise,
   here's the lock to fit the key:

fourteen letters in a word
   may seem frankly alien;
yet the word's not so absurd…
   it's 'sesquipedalian!'

Habeas Corpus

Habeas corpus –
　he's our man;
if we can't have him,
　nobody can!

Hurly-Burly

Hurly-Burly's one sly guy –
   wears his cap and gown awry;
plots his pleasure (he ain't shy!)
   like a six-pack samurai.

Our man Hurly's quite a wit
   when he dares to err a bit;
once he's packed and stowed his kit,
   Burly likes to kick some lit.

Poetry is Hurly's game –
   he thinks prose-*artistes* are lame;
verse is how he shoots at fame
   (when and *if* he cares to aim).

Burly says that bland's just *grand*
   when he hides his maestro's hand
orchestrating contraband
   for the sandbox *and* the sand.

Nothing bothers our man Burl' –
   least of all, a bad referral;
neither boor nor cad nor churl
   wants to toy with *this* guy's girl.

Now that Burly's gone to bed –
   just like you, retirèd –
schemes abound in his young head
   reamed in black and white…and red!

I Often Think I'd Like To Be

I often think I'd like to be
   that bee that I could never be—
bewitching as the case should be
   to be a bee, or not to be.

This—my being just a bee—
   is what beguilement might be:
as bees in flight appear to be
   bedazzled just to be a bee.

I Wonder, Shall I Ever See...

I wonder, shall I ever see
   a tree that grows defiantly?
And if I do, what will I say
   to limbs that crash to earth that day?

That *present* is as things must be;
   or *past,* what may no longer be?
That *future* is what still can be
   if pith enough there be in ye?

But what of lightning, drought and cold—
   catastrophes—can these be told
to leaves that freely call decay
   a thing of which those limbs might say:

that *present* is as things must be;
   and *past,* what may no longer be;
or *future:*   what can only be
   if sap does not abandon ye?

If Birds Could Swim

If birds could swim
   and fish could fly,
and you, the Apple
   of my eye,

might grant to me
   a final wish,
I'd only ask
   for more of fish.

For fishing's deep
   (or so they say)
as they creep off
   and let us stay

to talk about
   what's in your head;
or why you doubt
   what's in your bed.

The latter is
   beyond advice;
as you well know,
   I've struck out twice.

 At once, I'd say,
   "Now stay the course—
and if today
   it's just remorse

you feel, I doubt
 you'll err as I
did, Apple of
 your father's eye."

If Only I Could Be a Slug

If only I could be a slug,
   I'd slump upon a Persian rug
of emeralds and threads of gold
   to save my slime from grime and cold.

And then, I'd make a dressing gown
   of clotted cream and chocolate brown
and crumbs set nattily adrift
   to give my fatty cells a lift

from which a slug might squeeze some wit,
   prepare a meal, imbibe a bit
while wondering what snails could do
   (if only they'd remember to).

But snails are far more apt to stay
   in bed to study leaf decay–
which must inexorably lead
   to shells that crack and go to seed

and render snails a wee bit slow
   to keep up with the bawdy show
of one bright slug whose brief request
   would give to both this manifest

of differences in what they do
   (if they can but remember to):
while snails stay slimed for raillery,
   young slugs are primed for thuggery.

Little Miss Muffet

Little Miss Muffet
 sat hard on her duff so it
wouldn't be ferried away.

Along came a stranger
 who cried out "No danger!"
to which she protested *"Parlez!"*

"I've just come to visit
 and couldn't resist it
when I saw you sitting that way."

"Then tell me your purpose
 that I might subvert it,"
said prodigy's young *protégée*.

"But Miss, I'm no misfit –
 now come, have a biscuit
as I've got some pretties today."

"This duff ain't no manger,
 and I ain't no babe, sir,
so get thee and thy myrrh away!"

"You're tough, little Muffet,
 and likely enough
to lay waste to my little buffet."

"You aren't a park ranger,
 and I'm not deranged, sir,
so no way should you stay, José!"

* * * * *

The gist of this story
  is nothing so boring
as what may or not come to play

at times when young girls,
  quite obsessed with their curls,
think nothing except to obey –

but rather, like Muffet,
  just tell them to stuff it
when strangers uncomfortably stray,

and disregard suitors
  who sail in on scooters
while paving the way with *'Olé!'*

Nolens Volens

My friend Nolens – just like me –
   goes to bed unwillingly.
Nolens thinks that sleep is rot;
   Mom, however, thinks it's not.

"What the heck," – I hear Nol say –
   "sleeping leads to tooth decay!"
Nolens has a point, I think;
   Mom, however, doesn't blink.

"Sleep's not right for guys like us –
   guys who spit and curse and cuss!"
Nol – it's clear – loves sacred texts;
   Mom politely genuflects.

Then, as *I'm* about to swear,
   I see Nolens grab his bear,
hibernate, and take a chair
   high up where there's no *there* there.
   Nolens's fingers, once asleep,
   leave off fleecing Bo Peep's sheep –
wherein I discern the rub:
   Nol has fallen for the cub.

I next grumble fitfully
   as the clock strikes half past three,
sinking me with each dull clink –
   Mom, however, doesn't shrink.
  She, instead, has darker plans:
    "Afternoons," she countermands,
"aren't – like mornings – made for naps;
   pillows take the place of laps."

Volens now unmasks my frown
   as Mom gently swings me down,
sending me between the sheets
   into rapture that entreats

me to ask for one more thing
   to divest of sleep its sting:
that while sucking on my thumb,
   I consider Nol my chum.

The Butcher, the Baker, the Candlestick Maker

The butcher, the baker, the candlestick maker
   had closed and gone home for the day.
Their lights were put out; their doors had been locked;
   and bankers quite liked them that way.

"Now, let us eat cake!" said the banker's young wife,
   but bakers had all gone away.
"So where is the meat that I need for my knife –
   or shall we dish fish up today?"

The butcher, the baker, the candlestick maker
   knew nothing of light until May;
but once the Depression was done with obsession,
   they clapped their caboodle in clay.

"Where *now* is our cake?" said the banker's young wife,
   suggesting that cake was okay –
except when a wife might envision a life
   in a boat, full of fish, in a bay.

The baker, the butcher, the candlestick maker
   had only what sailors might say
about the receding of one banker's pleading
   while wee little wife sailed away.

Time Runs the Boldest of Races

Time runs the boldest of races:
   when off on a quest to discover the best,
Time sets the slowest of paces.

Time solves the coldest of cases:
    while flashing a grin from its diligent chin,
Time scoops the story it chases.

Time questions **SOLD!** in old places:
   if what we don't know has the pretense of show,
Time looks on down at its laces.

Time owns the wisest of faces:
   TKO'ed in the ring; up with skylarks in spring;
    singing out; staying put; sipping milk; slugging gin;
(Time looks to cover all bases.)

"Who Do Dat Voodoo?"

"Who do dat voodoo?"
   "I don't do; do you?"
"Not voodoo or hoodoo;
   dat hoodoo does *Dieu*."

"Dat hoodoo *is* voodoo
   or haven't you heard?"
"That's etymologically
   dumb and absurd!"

"Let's look at your hoodoo,
   you fatuous bird:
if 'hoodoo' and 'voodoo'
   derive from one word,

then I'm a canary,
   and you're just a cave
not even binary
   equations can save;

as hoodoo *or* voodoo
   in d'Alembert's game
would take what investors
   might bet on a name

and turn it to profit
   or force it to starve
and pocket whatever
   its bones leave to carve.

Ubiquitous Brown Birds

Maybe they're the *summum bonum* –
   best and brightest feathered nerds.
Just the same, who'd want to clone 'em:
   these ubiquitous brown birds?

Little else would dare replace them
   – can a bird outrace a bee? –
notwithstanding space to grant 'em
   e pluribus ubiquity.

Potpourri or Pot pourri

A Letter to My Mother

Hallo one last time, dearest mother of mine,
   I trust that you're keeping my bed
as white as our birches; as starched as our pine;
   as clear as our sky overhead.

The rumour now runs: my old mother misses
   some devil—apparently me.
That devil, in truth, remembers her kisses,
   her ratty old coat and her tea.

Some evenings, I'll wager, the vision's perverse:
   a tavern; your boy in a brawl
with sailors whose cunning eviscerates; worse:
   his entrails spill script on a wall.

Now pause for a moment to think this one through;
   and tell me I've failed to comply
to wend my way homeward, awarded by you
   with kisses that cause me to fly.

I think rather not—and trust you'll make haste
   to give this old rumour the lie.
The truth is I'm homesick and don't want to waste
   one more swinish night in this sty.

In spring, I'll come running back home to your arms
   outstretched, bearing handfuls of sage,
provided we separate clocks from alarms,
   and you get a grip on my age—

then leave me to suffer my hedonist's binge
   of wine-baited women and song,
the better to serve them my head on a fringe
   of lace—as they've asked all along.

But please don't suggest that redemption and grace
   can somehow be gotten by prayer;
you are the steeple I mount for the chase,
   the lady I take to the fair.

So, empty your pail full of nettles and needs,
   and don't let our dacha grow cold;
and toss out your ratty old coat with its beads;
   then, Mom, let's rekindle the bold!

ПИСЬМО К МАТЕРИ

Ты жива еще, моя старушка?
Жив и я. Привет тебе, привет!
Пусть струится над твоей избушкой
Тот вечерний несказанный свет.

Пишут мне, что ты, тая тревогу,
Загрустила шибко обо мне,
Что ты часто ходишь на дорогу
В старомодном ветхом шушуне.

И тебе в вечернем синем мраке
Часто видится одно и то ж:
Будто кто-то мне в кабацкой драке
Саданул под сердце финский нож.

Ничего, родная! Успокойся.
Это только тягостная бредь.
Не такой уж горький я пропойца,
Чтоб, тебя не видя, умереть.

Я по-прежнему такой же нежный
И мечтаю только лишь о том,
Чтоб скорее от тоски мятежной
Воротиться в низенький наш дом.

Я вернусь, когда раскинет ветви
По-весеннему наш белый сад.
Только ты меня уж на рассвете
Не буди, как восемь лет назад.

Не буди того, что отмечталось,
Не волнуй того, что не сбылось, -
Слишком раннюю утрату и усталость
Испытать мне в жизни привелось.

И молиться не учи меня. Не надо!
К старому возврата больше нет.
Ты одна мне помощь и отрада,
Ты одна мне несказанный свет.

Так забудь же про свою тревогу,
Не грусти так шибко обо мне.
Не ходи так часто на дорогу
В старомодном ветхом шушуне.

9/11/03

    (to Debra P.)

As we tonight stood gawking
   out at leathered chicks still hawking
(less the means and will for stalking)
   tricks on phones,
I rebounded when you touched me,
   like a bell relieved of belfry
up in towers set to dip
   down deep in stones.

Then like sailors high on sailing
   and indifferent to the wailing
of some fishermen foully scaling
   skin from bones,
we spoke of politics' eclipse,
   and of how men would use your hips
in hopes of finding happiness
   in deadbeat zones.

Still bemused, I went on thinking
   about shattered towers shrinking
down like beasts of burden sinking
   under groans,
till my eyes caught yours, hard shuttered,
   and my lips sought yours, but stuttered,
and I felt my pique emit
   in measured moans.

When you refrained from weeping
   for the *names* now roundly sleeping,
names once happy merely keeping
   heat in homes,
I looked up as you stood screening
   out the sordid sounds of keening
down where Jonestown junkies mewled
   like metronomes.

Now I'm sitting here reflecting
   like some ruined rogue neglecting
one heart's need to go collecting
   unpaid loans,
as I contemplate my stuttering
   from within a belfry shuttering
out the knell of hell that first-blush love
   intones.

A Body May With Wit Rebel

A body may with wit rebel,
    claim fame and quit the earth,
then ride a star-struck carousel
    right back to humble birth.

But with the tolling of a bell
    to mark that body's worth,
Death opens wide the gates of hell
    to catacombs of mirth.

A Poet Writes in Silence

A poet writes in silence,
    but in silence finds a lash
to whip from words compliance
    and beat out the balderdash.

A poet hails each palsied verse
    with wit and drunken cheer,
then looks to hire a sober hearse
    to chugalug its bier.

A poet fills his cud with chew
    and lets it set a while,
as nothing short of spit will do
    to macerate his bile.

A poet takes from prose a word
    – as any pirate will –
then cuts his booty to a third
    and brings it home to kill.

An Acorn's Got a Heritage

An acorn's got a heritage,
   and *oak*'s its patronymic,
which blokes write off as parentage
   reduced to 'demonymic.'

Though *Quercus* is a family name
   whose roots suggest *vulgaris,*
no etymological legerdemain
   can dupe a good Thesaurus.

The grunt in us may simply wish
   to find a place and claim it –
though Hamilton (the III of Fish)
   might erringly still frame it.

What's in a name, if after all
   the hullabaloo, it sticks?
Do roses not return in fall
   with one new crop of pricks?

And so it was with Hamilton,
   through sticks and stones devoted
to unknown soldiers ushered in
   and to their graves demoted.

"Some have at first for Wits, then Poets past, Turn'd Criticks next, and prov'd plain Fools at last; Some neither can for Wits nor Criticks pass, As heavy Mules are neither Horse or Ass."

—Alexander Pope

Any Dope Can Write a Ditty

Any dope can write a ditty
   without pity, without hope;
and yet few surpass the witti-
   ness of Alexander Pope.

Short on grit, he'd often deftly
   denigrate with eloquence,
hoping he could hook a hefty
   lefty with benevolence.

Let me "live, unseen, unknown," &
   "unlamented," let me die.
Solitude, with wit, cemented
   Pope's relentless slam on wry.

Any dope can write a ditty,
   Scriblerous, and lacking hope;
only one could write as wittily
   as Alexander Pope.

Blizzard

While all the world's awash in white,
   like one bright Motel 6er,
I run myself a bubble bath
   and add some warm elixir.

But first, I watch as birds bound out
   like junkies to a fixer,
and then rush back, incensed, to bark
   in loud refrain: "You *dick*, Sir!"

In this young bunch, I have a hunch
   – if not for one old geezer –
that any *coq* could hook a hen
   with sock-in-beak to tease her.

A spawn spreads out upon the lawn,
   then ruts inside the gutter—
an exhibition, seemingly,
   a "Halt!" from me could shutter.

I watch as doves, with shoulders hunched,
   now bunch abreast and cower;
but unlike *quid pro* wails of quail,
   doves' *quo* trades quip for glower.

Le jazz au bar sends out a wire-
   less love song to my shower,
just as a clutch of jays essays
   to sack a seedless flower.

If ever you were keen to know
   how days can waste a critter,
you'd merely need to watch the ways
   that snowbound birds can fritter.

Busted!

The dusk drops down like curtains on your coastline,
   while seagulls scream in rank obscenity.
The sands of time now sift only for surfers
   who stand to ride this poet's parody.

Those Hessians you once hired all stand shell-shocked,
   perhaps because their *putsch* means poverty.
I would've thought the Swiss made better soldiers,
   with bellies full, they'd guard officiously.

You held too long to an image ill-begotten,
   which now, like paint, insults your vanity
just as one captious sun, one moon insouciant,
   announce, through smirks, your pointless piety.

For all your hymns to stardust and the ocean,
   it's not *your* name we see on that marquee;
so take a spin – go strutting down the boardwalk;
   the salt air's just the cure for anomie.

With luck, you'll find another duned companion,
   a chum in ersatz camaraderie,
who'll lend to you his own good bones as cushion,
   and pick your nits while humming do-re-mi.

Now off with you to find life's last real pleasures:
   a solid bed; a mate of some esprit;
a night's bright wine, whose one cup wants refilling;
   and then, as dawn yawns pink, some thin, brown tea.

'Caned and Disabled

You wanna fuck with me? Come fuck with me.
   It don't make no damned difference.
You wanna keep on fucking me?
   Okay, let's split the difference.

You think I like the shit you do?
   Get real, dude, note this difference:
that thing you do is what *I* do
   much better, with *in*difference.

You wanna call me 'mother' now?
   There's just a little difference.
Your mother cares – which I do not.
   You cool with that small difference?

You wanna call me 'system' then?
   First learn to tell the difference:
you fuck with me; I'll fuck with you.
   You feel the little difference?

The rich ride out; the poor duck down;
   to *me,* there ain't no difference.
It's how I clean the gene pool *up*
   that lastly splits the difference.

If some return, and some do not,
   should I regret the difference?
With brand-new beachfront property,
   does FEMA fret the difference?

So let's come clean, get to the point:
   your species makes no difference.
I'm motherfucking Nature, stooge.
   Do you *now* get the difference?

If not, then simply get a clue
   should ends still make a difference:
omega – like *extinct* – is where
   your 'fucking' makes no difference.

Coitus

I love to coït with you at dawn –
   not to fuck and not to screw.
The one's a thing they do to you;
   the other, a thing too many do
(that many would do better to eschew).

I love to coït with you at night –
   eyes to eyes, both pairs wide open
while we quiver under sliver of moonlight.
   'Pornography,' you say, 'is a public tumble in the sheets,
a public spectacle of meats, grinding obvious.'
   'Pornography,' *I* say, 'is a none-too-gentle wrestle
of two bodies, both of which want not to be.'

I love to coït with you mid-morning:
   our tummies rumble full of eggs.
You, softer than the wildest grasses,
   that mound of thyme between your legs
I tease; while climbing up my spine, your toes
   outstretched like crampons snug to bones,
I beg: 'Come, higher still, and coil;
   climb my back and rake me under!'

But most of all,
   I love to coït with you at lunch:
through a long and lusty moment
   we stretch out into an hour,
when the public's all awash in self-applause –
   all mistaken with itself,
all betaken by its stealth,
   fairly duped in innuendo,
quite beguiled by clickety-claque,
   you and I absconding
with a lay out on the lawn,
   with a poke up in the attack,
with a boink behind the stack.

The day is done – now back to dawn.

Diminished Expectations

While once we pirated deep in pink,
   and randomly ravaged in red,
a collared conscript hauled us back,
   with all our passions bled
to shades of violate
   and pillaged, bloodless love.

In haste and fast-paced revelry,
   we played our giddy game,
as if one brief parade of sparks
   could conjure up a flame;
then came September –
   to snuff out summer love.

Remember how our silly scheme,
   relieved of sober thought,
when first exposed to scrutiny,
   then shunned the object sought
till we recanted
   and blamed that checkered love?

But think of all the letters kept
   that fantasies might last;
of pages drafted easily –
   yet easily recast – for eyes
once eager, then glazed
   like porcelain love.

Now each day climbs up on a saddle
   with countenance cast in shame,
remanding in its gross triage
   the limbless hours and lame:
smart soldiers *once* of cavalry,
   those hours riding through,
in uniform and purposeful,
   in shining contrast to
this thing called love –
   this bland redoubt,
this bootless love.

Epilogue to a *Splendid* Love Affair

Why should I call our bed *sanctum sanctorum*,
   if 'holy' is a handle I abhor –
while you, who'd say that dogs fuck with decorum,
   think love is just another word for war?

How clearly I can see you in the trenches,
   your lips grown strangely limpid with the gore
of lads once taking turns upon the benches –
   mere youths who'd put to shame a bugle corps.

If here I sit, long after battle, wreathing
   our armistice in ribbons on the floor,
it's only to observe your measured breathing,
   as you set pegs for one more paramour.

But trust me, doll: I'm anything but eager
   to watch you test another little score
of boys whose private parts you'd now beleaguer –
   just tufts of cotton candy to a whore.

And lastly, keep in mind that tricks cost double
   when forced to see the light of day at four –
an hour at which your bed would bounce like rubble,
   if only rams could batter down your door.

Family Planning

Though you and I are litter-free,
   you shake the dust from stars for *three*.
Why do I then procrastinate?
   Try gamely to extrapolate.

Two is ardent; *two,* complete;
   (it's the sum of us: four feet).
But *two* is nature's sinecure –
   an office you cannot endure.

I appeared to you distracted
   at the moment you contracted,
and to pause at your request
   that I investigate a breast.

When you then once protracted
   what I'd cannily retracted,
I heard you crassly snicker "steer"—
   so, bullied up my *bullish* gear.

You say lovers owe to science
   what you coyly call *compliance.*
I want races through wet places;
   you, to buy us an oasis.

We're (1) long on motives; (2) without means;
   (3) keen on votives; (4) short on beans.
If what you want's a family,
   then let's just buy a dog.

Flight 103 to Lockerbie: Happy Anniversary!

I have a quiet storm outside my window;
   it's weather, pure and simple, just release.
Are these the gales that tore the skies of Scotland
   then showered down her children, piece by piece?

This bit of storm, quite spent, is now reclining
   upon my house, turned inward from the sea.
Our naked coast lies warm and under cover
   of snow-drift sheets sent down from Lockerbie

'cross Galloway and Dumphries' frozen meadows,
   through Strathclyde, lashing heathers down below
as desperately, the Channel tries appealing
   to waves that riffle flame-retardant snow.

You see, my bit of storm is simple comfort;
   my children lie beside me on the floor.
I'm not that mother rocking still at daybreak
   with hopes on hinges, staring at the door.

From Dust We Come, to Dust We Go

From dust we come, to dust we go,
   like rednecks in a rodeo.
If once or twice along the way,
   we stumble, or our horses stray,

it's not our dust that stops the show –
   as horses, unlike folks, bestow
decorum upon majesty,
   while we trot out our travesty.

So take it easy, take it slow,
   and take to heart what little glow
may radiate from one cold urn
   in which life's nettles slowly burn.

If nothing comes of all you know,
   or what your wildest seeds might sow,
then auction off your last remains;
   take your losses; stake your gains.

I Like the Haze of Summer Days

I like the haze of summer days
   through lenses cut for fall,
which like some lazy lizard's gaze
   crawls down my bedroom wall

to spare us both the brazen light
   of one bright billiard hall,
where spiders fight—and then invite—
   rude lizards to a brawl.

But if some spider starts to graze
   upon my bedroom wall,
I'll scream for days and lizards' ways
   to help me end it all

(though wonder, too, how spiders snooze
   while under some cat's paw,
and if in haste they fling *"J'accuse!"*
   to wrest a caterwaul)

as caterpillars seek romance
   and frenzied lizards crawl
like lambs to slaughter, both to dance
   at spring's Arachno Ball.

I Like the Orange, but *Love* the Black

I like the orange,
   but *love* the black
of summer skies
   that drift on back

to pick the bones
   of winter's rack
upon whose spikes
   fall likes to stack

the shoots and leaves
   of last spring's snack
until fall cleans
   the wretched wrack

of spring's entrails
   and summer's slack
in time for winter's
   cataract

or Halloween's
   now empty sack—
whose orange rictus
   mocks the lack

of harlequins
   in winter's shack—
and then in remonstrance,
   laughs back.

I Miss Her Most in Winter

I missed her first in fall, when the moon stood off alone,
   and the stars arrived like gangsters at her doorstep;
I missed her even more, when the earth began to swoon
   in the darkness that made light of her abduction.

I missed her once again, when the sun could only cower,
   when her Swedish sun slipped down below horizon;
I missed her even more, when the icebergs cut and flowed,
   and the sea commenced to froth in cold abandon.

I missed her often, too, when the snow at night subsided,
   and the trees in their reprieve stood out like top hats;
I missed her even more, when her Northern Lights collided,
   and the stars fell back to earth like powdered sugar.

But I miss her *most* of all, when this winter's winds recall,
   how we'd lie beneath her covers in Elyseum;
And the lie is underscored, when that once grave moon of fall
   now limns this: our former love – turned mausoleum.

I Prowl About My Garden

I prowl about my garden on
    a lion-tamer's dare:
self-rusticated, put upon,
    devoutly debonair;

then crawl on back to maul the fact
    of how old lions think,
while wondering (despite the tact
    of crouching on the brink

of craziness that lions know
    without a lioness),
what wild oats I might yet sow
    before I obsolesce.

Then off I go to paw the bed
    for one last goodnight kiss,
until it dawns on me you're dead—
    oblivious of this.

I Remember When I Was a Player

I look at the field; I look at the court;
   I look at the pool; I look at my bed;
and remember – when I was a player.

I look overhead as an airplane ascends,
   and then I look out as mere *children* descend
to the subway – with someplace to go.

I look at my drink alongside my butts;
   I look at my face – then wish I had not;
and I hear how much 'prayer' sounds like 'player.'

I look at a girl; I look at my boy;
   I note how that girl then looks at my boy;
and remember – how I, too, was a player.

I stare at my feet, then look at my hands;
   I pick up a pen, and shuffle a page;
and then try to wonder – if I'm still a player.

I Rummage 'Round in My Safe Place

I rummage 'round in my safe place
   of wistful rustication,
and watch as stars wink back from space
   too weak for exclamation.

Here, branches dangle little socks
   of buds in consternation
at winter's still insistent knocks
   and spring's equivocation –

till sultry summer calls on cue
   to brood about her station,
and autumn gripes, yet muddles through
   her fall from adulation.

Each season has its cross to bear –
   then when it's lost, vexation;
yet lest we think their lot unfair,
   they, too, all take vacation!

I Watch a Spider Spin Her Web

I watch a spider spin her web
   and wonder: What's the play?
as like a camera-wise celeb,
   she keeps her prey at bay.

If 'laughable' describes her knack
   for fretting straight-laced paths,
I may suggest a sober snack
   on cream of pickled Plaths –

as Sylvia was not averse
   to phrases turned askew;
and so, would patronize her purse
   by paying dad his *du*.

Now, 'predatory' captures best
   my bats on belfry days
persisting – unlike bells at rest –
   in wringing out the ways

that sound damnation might relieve
   a life of lettered dross
while spidermaids upbraid their weave
   of deftly fettered floss.

I Wonder, Does a Tree Look Down?

I wonder: does a tree look down
   upon its trunk and think
how days before – or was it years –
   its roots began to sink?

I wonder, too, as I reflect
   upon my desk and ask
of pens for which no paper waits:
   is life too great a task?

If work is such a willful act
   not needing any goad,
what right have I to dignify
   my lot as overload?

And then, at last, I wonder what
   most poetry contains,
if in it neither will to live
   nor coquetry obtains.

I've Swooned to Sweet, Yet Scented Sour

I've swooned to sweet, yet scented sour,
   and hoped that hands might tell the hour
in which I'd have my cake and eat it, too.

To wit, my blush turned middling blue
   as, bit by bit, our want fell due
and took from us—you, bride; me, groom—our bower.

Now, brides may spurn a wilted flower,
   and grooms may turn to grave from dour.
In short, the two rise up, sink down, move through

to demonstrate that only you
   may gather up both wool and glue,
then leave to weave another, better bower.

If Love is to Cartography What Romance is to Maps

If love is to cartography
   what romance is to maps,
then both could use some carpentry
   to bridge their little gaps.

As once upon a humbler time,
   when labor ran this town,
and one week's wages sounded fine
   to buy the wife a gown,

it wasn't love – unused to maps
   for markets or corrections –
that traded up in sugar-snaps
   to power down objections,

but workers, who would right each wrong
   in gaps from *both* directions
as one fell short, the other long,
   to zero out defections.

In re: End of Days

The living-room's broom-swept; all glasses clean and dry
   and moved to private cellars, locked and separate.
Only bitter wine remains, the sweet gone wry.
   So, help me with the guest-list – date indefinite.

We have been civil in our separating ways –
   a study case and really quite commendable –
nothing less than neighborly, amenable
   to what may pass for two last grand hurrays.

We could open up the curtains, not yet bundled;
   but these are down and folded, put away.
We might dance upon the carpet, not yet trundled,
   to stop the clock. I wonder: would you stay?

We could walk the garden perfectly suspended.
   But then, with weeds unchecked, why go that way?
Have we ever thought to walk *that* walk untended,
   to do as other lovers gone astray?

We will *never* sweep the halls again together;
   nor speak again of love that once behooved,
nor waste some spendthrift time among the heather;
   nor even walk the garden, now removed.

Stand for one last family photo? I don't think so.
   Should I ask to sign the book a fine 'farewell'?
Then I must ask: how fine? how fair? how well?
   In irony, I ask – and yet I know.

Indeed, it's time to split the gas and the electric,
   since it's now about the cash and nothing more.
Then part withal and go our separate ways
   on this – our end of days together.

It's Time To Do the Christmas Cards

It's time to do the Christmas cards
    and dig up last year's trove
of God-forsaken Abélards
    now destined for the stove.

Who wrote? Who didn't,
    but probably couldn't?
(The business of Christmas
    must always be gay!)

Triage is often hardest when
    two thirds of what we've drunk
thinks only of how Héloïse
    might save us from a funk.

Who sent? Who didn't?
    Who might've, but couldn't?
Who should've — not really —
    but did anyway?

Our verses are a pocketful
    of pennies much too slim
to purchase what's canonical
    of bros named aptly 'Grimm.'

Who gets? Who doesn't?
    Who died? Who didn't?
Who hijacked "Hosanna!" —
    then called it a day?

Love Becomes You in the Fall

We're easily teased by seasons and their vigor,
   whose pique would leave us scratching in delight.
But with the itch of ink and blood receding,
   the scab of reason leads us back to night.
The mood, I think, is done for frantic pleading –
   and so, I ask, why stoop to stop it all?
The truth, my darling, let's accept:
   that love – the heady pace of it – becomes you in the fall.

The spring requires no imagination,
   while summer hangs indifferent in the breeze.
And if, in winter, you throw off the covers
   – since quilts (all unpaid lovers) fail to please –
that leaves one season ripe for rumination.
   Would you deny us just to skew it all?
A wrong, my dear, let's now redress,
   for love – the curious grace of it – becomes you in the fall.

A slipshod youth in love with provocation
   despises ocean, laughs at simple sand.
And so, the weightless end is sheer amusement:
   to wander out to sea or die on land.
But with the years come fears of isolation.
   Would you eschew *us* to escape it all?
The dread, my darling, let's admit:
   that love – the weathered face of it – becomes you in the fall.

Till now, you've never wanted for affection –
   as ties restored the *earthly* to "delight"
and bliss rekindled animal addiction
   to that sweet pain that pulled you left and right
into the arms of odd, assorted lovers.
   Would you now drop *us* to pursue it all?
Your sin (enchanting!) let's confess:
   that love – the ardent chase of it – still haunts you in the fall.

Love in Winter Storage

My love goes lurking like a sparrow
   attached to nervous springs,
who takes each seed and water bead
   as sweetmeat meant for kings.

My love goes squealing like a squirrel,
who fidgets and then flings
the grains he steals from birds beset
   by mad cats wanting wings.

My love goes burrowing – a worm,
   who dirt for dowry slings;
and thus he builds a squalid mound
   to which his harem clings.

My love goes languishing, like laurel:
   with roots asleep, she sings
from now till spring a sullen song
   whose rune retreats in rings.

MAD* Mongers

Each time, outgunned, we'd set a sail
   so much like fools, prepared to fail,
though not without first loading up to fire;
   then bending low with flags aloft,
we'd listen as the roar ran oft
   as words will do – content to just retire.

Then once again when spleen had passed,
   we'd pick up pieces, staunch the blast
of blood and bile and ballast, all upended.
   We'd take the spillage of a season,
shuck the shame and ransom reason,
   build ourselves a new wall, stopgap-mended.

So was our love: it ground hardcore
   through every fight, a bloody bore;
we'd rot in trenches, desperate for solutions.
   We *could* go on – the wounds congealed;
yet scarred, I could no longer feel
   your once hard body, soft in resolutions.

If now you sometimes miss the sound
   of our two children, dreamward-bound,
repeating prayers to keep their nightmares shallow.
   The candle's out; our ground is dry;
so give no further thought to try
   to conjure crops from fields that now lie fallow.

When sleep comes hard at new moon's phase,
   you might consider all the ways
that winds can pass without once bending willow.
   And sometimes, too, *I'll* sit, reflect,
with finger-thoughts upon your neck,
   how once it filled the hollow of my pillow.

* Mutually Assured Destruction

March Snow

I fall too late for Christmas past,
   and feel cast out in spring;
if I can claim one saving grace,
   it's that I've learned to cling

to sidewalks no one wants to clean,
   and gutters just for kicks;
I'm like those pilot episodes
   that no TV can't fix

until next snowy Christmas Eve
   when Hell bends Lent for Hallmark,
and both fly skyward in reprieve –
   like some absurdist aardvark

which then like birds now sitting tight
   upon my empty feeder,
looks once at me, then once at night
   and thinks to call it sieder.

My Pears, My Port and My Stilton

Many seek limos, champagne and the Hilton;
   I'll take my pears, my port and my Stilton.
Others crave villas, châteaux or a manor;
   I'm quite at home with a stoop and a banner.

Nothing delights like a sandwich and pickle;
   I can get both—less the meat—for a nickel.
Some get a kick out of dates at the Hilton;
   I'd rather pick at my pears, port and Stilton.

Free am I now to ignore the odd rent-hike,
   given my barter of home for a trail bike.
Equally free to ignore what's in season,
   since it's decidedly well beyond reason.

Little can dampen a wry disposition
   once disabused of its old-school tradition.
Nor could a trick flick my Bic® at the Hilton,
   lest she be packing some pears, port and Stilton.

Narcissus Meets Echo at the Weeping Well

"You would now trade," a voice cries up,
   "your moon-bright night for me?"
"Not yet," I say, "I still crave light
   to find the one loved me."

"Is she not gone?" that voice now brays
   like rasps on irony.
"She came; she looked; we reflected;
   then cooed in symmetry."

"Such love should know a sticking point!"
   voice says in mockery,
till well's rank cant falls back to earth
   in thrall to gravity.

"She bade me sing," I call within,
   "a hymn to Coventry.
So I obliged and rained like bombs
   in hard-shelled mimicry."

"And now you try to cobble words?"
   voice cackles captiously.
"As if with tea and tepid prose
   you might win sympathy?"

"A man," I say, "should not be shrill –
   it sullies sonnetry;
but may, instead, let iambs rage
   in reciprocity."

"If now she came, could you hold back,
   like dikes detaining sea?"
"She cannot come. She never was,
   nor is, nor yet shall be."

Not Enough

I sit in your swing on a late-summer day.
   It creaks from disuse, the board warped, the ropes frayed.
This swing, I made once, with hammer and nails.
   In this swing, you swung once, with playthings in pails.
Not enough, quite simply, not enough, I'm afraid.
   So now, I sit here alone.

I lie in your hammock on a late-summer day.
   It smells of mildew, rotted leaves and decay.
This hammock, I hung once, with hooks from a tree.
   From this hammock, you tilted at windmills and me.
Not enough, quite simply, not enough, I'm afraid.
   So now, I lie here alone.

I browse near your pond on a late-summer day.
   A pond of spun green and gold strings on display.
This pond, I dug once, with muscle and spade;
   for your eyes, for your feet, to feed and to wade.
Not enough, quite simply, not enough, I'm afraid.
   So now, I browse here alone.

I stare at your table on a late-summer day.
   Its planks split, struts undone, dark and damp from the rain.
This table, I laid once, with lanterns at play.
   At this table, you ate once, held lions at bay.
Not enough, quite simply, not enough, I'm afraid.
   So now, I stare here alone.

I stand in your room on a late-summer day.
  Dumbly hanging, unblinking, their strings full of webs,
are the puppets I brought you as boodle in laces,
  then hung them aloft to keep watch from dark places.
Not enough, quite simply, not enough, I'm afraid.
  So now, I stand here alone.

Now, Where Would the First Wind Begin?

Now, where would the first wind begin,
   and what of the sails it would bend,
if much like the wages of sin,
   the start loses sight of the end?

And why would it even begin
   if hurricanes merely portend
a thriller in tonic and gin
   that idles, like sails, in the mend?

Out of a Rock, *NOW!*

In the druse of a rock, in a bed by a stream,
   I remember how we'd plan, and I relish how we'd scheme,
search for sloughs in the rock, slither down upon a beam,
   and without a worry split through the cracks to a dream,

grab an axe as we'd grind, stave a cradle as we'd scheme,
   go for gold in the rock, hew a groove in the beam,
sinking down, as we lay, melding mettle to our dream
   of a roof overhead, made of slate, by a stream.

Then we culled through the rock as we mulled on the beam,
   grating hard – as we cooed in our cote of a dream
under roof, without rules, in a swale by a stream –
   at the stones that would channel us like weirs through our scheme,

thinking too, as we grew in the drama of our dream
   – while it slid like a rill to a freshet to a stream –
that for babes out of lock, we'd need wedding in our scheme
   and to glom to the rock like a burl to a beam.

* * * * * * * * *

In the druse of a rock, in a glade by a stream,
   I regret how your act blew to smithereens our scheme,
and how I, like a crag, cracked the sinew of the beam,
   as from there, we then crashed through the cracks of our dream.

Roulette

(a lesson for my children)

You are, grave girl, my daughter,
   and you, brave boy, my son.
What once we thought a slaughter,
   we played on black—and won.

From a first orgasmic token
   till all of us lie dead,
our thread shall not be broken,
   nor aught of it gainsaid.

Your sperm are mine, once looted
   by one insurgent egg,
whose feet I bound and booted
   before she could renege.

A lash to my libido,
   the splash of it *posthaste;*
some mad and bad albedo,
   élan vital to taste.

You are, brave boy, my soldier,
   and you, grave girl, my sun.
As games of chance grow bolder,
   now play on red—and *run!*

SAD* Saps

We hustle through the middle months,
   oblivious of rut
beneath the moon of equinox,
   whose beams benight us – but

it's time to see the race renewed
   as we set off for solstice,
where darker days will soon occlude
   whatever habits hold us.

If then I gravitate too much
   to things that make you ill,
let's not, like lunatics, fly off
   to things we want to kill!

The daylight gapes as evening drapes
   her arms across my chest,
and pries from me a prurient swoon
   bestirring Bowdler's best

to expurgate the bawdy bits
   that whet our weary whims,
as burly winter scarifies
   and surly summer skims

the fat from feisty equinox
   to leave her body bare,
alone to sway—a castaway
   cut off from autumn's care

or spring's attempt to countermand
   crude summer's rude request:
that winter's wine-roused watchmen
   get *acquainted* with their guest.

* **SAD** = Seasonal Affective Disorder

"Screwered"

Chase the *chay* from Chardonnay
   and quit the *aq* from Aquavit.
And then, we'll just self-medicate
   with straws and Champagne split.

Benumbed, we'll stare at coasters
   since we're both profoundly lit,
like a pair of roiled roasters
   skewered tightly to a spit.

I delight to see you bluffing,
   though I know it's not your style.
In truth, you'd rather grab new stuff,
   than charm *me* with a smile

And while your age condones your rage
   to berth with *younger* barge,
I wonder: do you think it sage
   with lovelies still at large?

So back to cardboard coasters
   to redress what doesn't fit
as we sit like white bread toasters,
   too devoid of wit to quit.

So, *This* Is How Old Forests Feel

So, *this* is how old forests feel –
   like scattered wood in fall
and soaked to the skin of one slick night,
   while soughing *Fuck it all!*

Yes, fall: when leaves' abandonment
   reminds me of the form
in which each tree rehearses death,
   obedient to the norm –

which leads me to another thought
   beneath my prison quilt:
can you revive our rites of spring
   without survivor's guilt?

In two days' time, I go to court,
   then may go back to jail,
since nothing short of razzmatazz
   behooves me to avail

myself of how burnt forests feel
   when matching wits with fall,
as even now, I will not kneel –
   perhaps my fatal flaw.

Spell Unbounded

We had a yard full of yarrow,
   a house full of hyssop,
and then, we had them no more.

We lined boxes with comfrey,
   dressed windows with woodruff;
and then we redressed them for war.

Jasmine, we ran to the rooftop,
   while roses restrained us in jail.
Your eyes – I covered with petals.

You'd been sage and bay and catnip, too.
   I, horehound, lovage, feverfew –
till winter laid waste to our vows.

Then snow had to fall;
   and fall it did;
and break it did
   the spell.

Stratifying the Stress

You rue the red in stop-signs,
   say it jolts your worldview,
yet salivate when that same red
   rocks on with white and blue.

You loathe when I go bingeing,
   say my whisky's not the best.
But Christ, what I would give to see
   your Ritalin take a rest!

You ride your soccer star to games
   in a galloping SUV,
then deign to give *my* son the reins
   to *wax* it for a fee.

My daughter just turned hooker
   while *your* darling's on some quest.
If ZIP code's proof of pedigree,
   why rave about the rest?

My means are fast diminishing,
   while yours just jog on through.
It's different kinds of shock and awe
   that now enrage us two.

Surrender

It was cold where I stood ranting
    till you offered me a shelter,
took me in and made me swelter till mid-morning.
    I tunneled down and trundled through,
probed your copper core and knew:
    stone-faced, you'd command I do your bidding.

When I became your convert,
    my conversion made you tremble –
though I writhed, I never railed against your tactic.
    I was your spindle, and you spun me,
while I whirled alone and wrestled
    through a solid hedge of nettle into flame.

But when I sought to own you,
    tried to plumb and then to mine you,
tried, in vain, to strip your craven core,
    against all the gods you raved,
so that no lamb could be saved
    by some charitable angel passing over.

You closed your eyes like callow youth,
    feigned a little love. In truth –
life's irony much reveled in our fiction;
    for once you'd staked and flagged me,
just as quickly did you bag me,
    like some trash upon some heap upon some floor.

But now I ask you: am I useful,
    lying quiet, keeping still
as a doormat, or upon it, just a stain?
    Call me feckless; call me fiend;
call me thug or call me dung;
    call me anything at all… but let me stay?

Your shop is closed; your door is shut.
    Now you rise and now you strut –
as contemptuous as a pirate pitching ballast –
    on down the hall, out to the porch,
to seek another's blazing torch
    as ever fresher revelations blight our pathos.

I've walked the dog and paid the rent.
    I give up – let's fold the tent.
If it must be, so it shall be, I'll move on.
    And though I can't be with you,
let me last of all beseech you –
    now *his* lover, to be liquorish till the end.

The Ethos of Capital-isthmus*

What pay is *this*? Some chit now long past due
to get us roundly up and out the door,
to squeeze a measly buck, scratch out the score,
and shuck, to gutted towns, our shell-shocked crew?
Like *hell* you'll clear us out and push us through,
demanding, time-cards swiped, we quit the floor
and not – like peevish children – scream for more,
but take our bullied selves elsewhere for brew!
I tell you, China's coast is far from clear;
and China's sum of us is no less dim.
So go now – take your cash where it may still
win hearts and minds indifferent to our cheer,
but will, no doubt, find skillful hands to trim
the scrim of your next threadbare, off-shore thrill.

* 'Kapitalismus' is German for 'capitalism.'

The Garden Lusts for Thrill Tonight

The garden lusts for thrill tonight
   yet let us judge it fair –
the trellis, birch and pottery,
   each hungry element, bare.

Hard winter's eye regards it now
   in cold, paternal stare,
stiff winter's hand upon it now
   stays rigid in repair.

Each seed lies dormant, dreaming spring,
   each shooting dream, a flare –
into this longest, darkest night
   to which each spring is heir.

Yet I prefer to ruminate,
   then rant in my despair,
while seeds grow restless, birches strain
   against my wretched glare.

The Last Rose of Summer

I droop, then drop my petals one by one
   in penitence for having loved the sun.
"Too much," you say? That's just a damned cliché –
   like *whacks* your children give you when you stray.

But first things first. This bloom must try to cope
   with upstart petals clinging to the hope
I'll spot in them some crummy little thing
   that might induce a *cuckoo* clock to sing

by hunkering down with thorns to get a fix
   on those who mark their prominence in pricks
and would reduce me in their mindless rage
   to kindling – unheard of in an age

when fires are a dread domestic chore
   that even middling dunderheads abhor.
And Love-lies-bleeding? Just some lame excuse
   for silt to bed a flower on the loose.

You could've plucked me in my gravid prime,
   but let me go to seed upon the vine
like some ill-gotten gain, some stolen kiss
   that aphids run amok affect to miss.

So now, before I ask, like Salomé,
   of Herod, for Herodias, a tray
to offer up my pistil to the sun,
   I'll shed for *you* my petals, one by one.

The Moon Is Just a Calculus

The moon is just a calculus
   of vain and vapid wants
that test a woman's abacus
   in adding up men's haunts.

And yet, her thinking may rebound
   if ridiculed on sight—
while men remain aloof, then turn
   around to fight for flight.

On walls, she'll sit, content to sigh
   and contemplate the throng
of candidates who calcify,
   as 'qualify' no long-

er wants the time it might yet take
   to say the words "I do"—
or throw a glance to let her make
   amends to Waterloo.

So, should a woman come to you
   in vulnerable guise,
take heart that by the morning, dew
   won't dampen any eyes.

The *Real* Object of Her Affection

Was not, nor is, nor yet shall be
   some piddling thing, too flagrantly
displayed for sale that she might buy,
   and by her purchase satisfy

the loss that only time will heal
   as *things*, in bulk, cannot anneal
the heart. To wit, regard our tart:
   who now with empty shopping cart

goes screeching down the aisle –
   to pick and pluck from every pile
a swatch of this, a scrap of that,
   like discount-addled acrobat

or coupon tatterdemalion,
   turned sales-struck abecedarian.
At which point, thoughts of quiddity
   are trumped by her cupidity

as frenzied cart goes all amuck,
   she's heartless, cartless, out of luck,
yet not disposed to hose the gloss
   off lips that merely lisp the loss

of matters that dictate her fate,
   hence, much too late to promulgate
some principle by which she might
   regain composure, quit the site

to take her shopping spree ashore
   where beaches long for nothing more
than Robinson, simplicity,
   a loaf of bread, a wedge of Brie

and thee – a Crusoe non-imposter,
   with whom she might then prosper,
and heed the need of hungry hearts,
   which can't be found in shopping carts—

Finis!

Lady Astor: "Winston, you're drunk!"
W. Churchill: "But I shall be sober in the morning and you, madam, will still be ugly."
Lady Astor: "Mr. Churchill, if you were my husband, I'd put poison in your tea."
W. Churchill: "Madam, if I were your husband, I'd drink it."

"The Weather is for Kids, You Know"

"The weather is for kids, you know,"
   said Lady Astor as she'd stand
with nothing more to tell or show
   than why her ladyship's so grand.

Ms. Astor wouldn't once eschew
   a parasol, as sunshine could
incite a percolating few
   to filter through the neighborhood.

"Umbrellas are not meant for *beaux!*"
   said Lady Astor, who'd command
that suitors seeking favors toe
   the line to better gauge the hand.

Ms. Astor would at *once* eschew
   a lover if he never could
subscribe to what Ms. Astor knew:
   that wealth withheld is love withstood.

There Are No Larks on Broadway

There are no larks on Broadway
   singing love songs to the mews,
as every backstreet pigeon knows
   that Reuters riffs the news.

The province once of winos
   swigging Thunderbird by fifths
now pays to Disney tribute and
   to Providence, His myths.

The buskers who would serenade
   its sidewalks for a dime
have paved the way for hucksters
   hawking ads that almost rhyme.

Pornographers, whose 'pliant art'
   drew clients from the 'burbs,
have left the Square to cater to
   a far more vile urge –

where money is the music
   and receipts are all the rage,
"the play is (not) the thing"
   that sage accountants like to stage.

Instead, we have a Square – no square –
   and clocks that pimp the time;
like Vegas, we're a monument
   to Mammon's quiet crime.

There's Nothing Left but Cigarettes

There's nothing left but cigarettes,
   yet cigarettes are fine
to stand the test or kill the rest
   of lust, regrets, and time.

However risible our ruse
   to call this love *divine,*
if you think cigarettes and booze
   can help refine the mime

of it, okay then. Let's just waste
   a bit of wit online
and call a halt to all this chaste-
   ly existential crime.

A cognac, too, might nicely do
   as substitute for wine
to batten down the best of you
   and fortify my rhyme.

They Say that 'Orange' Has No Pair

They say that 'orange' has no pair,
    to which I answer "claptrap!"
since crosses are the things I bear –
    as eunuchs bear a satrap.

If one can militate in strophes
    with wit and reasoned ire,
then take your academic oaths
    and shove them up your pyre.

And so –

a proud Pierre stooped low to bow
    while slaughtering a sacred cow:
"L'orange a calculé ses chances,
    en robes pourprées, de faire romance."

Young Rilke pried the fruit apart
    and pulled a couplet from its heart:
"Apfelsinnen sinnen nicht,
    sei es denn aus Liebespflicht."

But Lorca kept *his* bulls at bay
    by seeing 'orange' in *"¡Olé!"*
"Naranjas son gillipollas,
    mientras que yo – cebollas."

The rest is one old history
    of how bold poets try to make
of citruses a mystery
    that only mistresses mistake.

Uneasy Traders

One loaf of fog I slip you:
   loaf – rugged, grey yet fair.
One teasing breath you whisper back,
   tense future hint of lips and hair.

One shelf of stars I throw you:
   coy, nipping at your courier moon.
One wanton touch you toss me back,
   stroke keen enough to make me swoon.

One undertow I catch you in:
   snarling tug on which you tumble.
One bracing word you hurl back,
   to block *my* fall, yet have me fumble.

One sheet of rain I wrap you in:
   sheet – warm and blue and spare.
One heavy sigh you sally back
   as wordless contract of repair.

All our longings and belongings
   titillate in taunt and tackle.
All our doubts and strange condolence
   strive to vitiate the shackle.

Waving Off the Last of Winter

Here lives a tree in league with me
   entombed through long, dark days.
It stands in niche like comfort quiche,
   plum hors-d'oeuvre to my gaze.

My indoor tree takes a catholic view
   and concludes it's all benign.
If outdoor rifts cause cosmic shifts,
   It can't be *her* design.

Across the road, the roofers pound,
   cajoling dogs to riot;
with slack-jawed tools like foul-mouthed fools,
   they squander Sunday's quiet.

Outside my window hangs the head
   of a lady in ceramic.
She looks at me through puckish lids
   and eyes that flirt with panic.

What Moon Are You!

What moon are you
   that I behold?
A laughing stock
   of grizzled mold

now waxing to
   a funny face,
yet shot quite through
   with cratered space?

You're very like
   the craven few
who promenade
   the avenue –

in orbits, all
   but nightly sold –
like legionnaires:
   once bold, now old.

What moon are you?
   I ask again –
as if an orb
   could give a damn

what I might ask
   or it might owe
in beams to those
   cast down below.

While Munching, I Muse on a Mural

(My thoughts upon first seeing the murals "Fantasy Scenes with Naked Beauties," by Howard Chandler Cristy—on the walls of THE LEOPARD (Restaurant) at des Artistes: 1 West 67th Street, NYC)

While munching, I muse on a mural—
   and wish that I had such a girl.
But having one got, and knowing she's not
   much more than a swinger I'd swirl,
I think I'll resist reviewing the list
   of what earns a girl a mural.

Now lunching, I glance at that mural,
   the subject of which is a girl
whose pubic delights invite me to bite
   my lip… that her curls might unfurl.
But furled they stay, respecting that lay-
   men venerate *art* in a mural.

Done lunching, I'm through with a mural
   that colors my thoughts of a girl.
But think: if in spring, I can loosen her string,
   she'll pop, like an oyster, a pearl—
as one brand of sand that always looks grand
   when flung at the feet of a mural.

While dining, I blink at my mural,
   which winks back at me like a girl,
as if to say "Go! Find your own little show
   where donkeys do girls for pearls"—
at which point I stand and sternly demand
   that vice police fleece this young mural!

Eldorado

I want to explore the globe of you
   one continent at a time.
I have no queen; I have no Isabella.
   I will not stake you with a flag.
I merely want to touch your beaches,
   swim your coves,
   feel your sands,
   sift the coasts of you,
one tender stroke at a time.

Not as prey, I swear, do I pursue you;
   I am no predator.
Nor do I search, or touch, or stretch to touch
   for glory or for queen.
I simply want to know
the feel of you,
   the pith of you,
   the pluck of you,
to share with all posterity.

You have forests; I am a ranger.
   You have swards; I am a warden.
You are of metal and things molten; I am a smith.
   I dream your harder parts,
but revel in your swampy regions.
   I kiss your ankles in ascent
towards summits still invisible.

I long to hear you, also smell you,
   chew upon your herbs and oils;
to savor every piece of you,
   the spices of your Hebrides.
To do, as tongues do – and taste
   the antipodes of you –
this much, and nothing more.

First, let me take you to that hill
   whence antlers grow and flowers spike;
where merry lusts to lusts by daybreak's fairest brim –
   like tumblers, startled skyward by night's broken fast,
all come windy down to chase away
   dawn's glum and sullen gatesmen –
we'll go, you and I, to see the still pale sun-limned scene.
   Night's gaudy splay of stars reclaimed,
her ribaldry now silenced,
   she'll cede that space to us;
like oven-baking bread – our chores ahead, all morning-bright.

Dawn broken. Dawn barely born.
   Dawn softly burnishing to steady light
first burst of morn. Yet swift enough to wrench
   with cries of sheer delight
that heady celebration of black night
   from all the glowworms rendered shy,
from all the fireflies turned idle.
   And then to loose that robe,
your robe, that hides, that chides
   your flesh to keep itself discreetly safe
and, from my own, quite separate.

I touch your vales, roam your miles,
   lean my cheek upon your slopes,
lie with you as pillow –
   you, now stripped bare, without coverlet or case.
Share with me your caves,
   your beds, your hills, your *terra firma*,
all flourishing, renewing, re-bounding
   like fallow deer – yet grave in orbit,
and in your fixëd place,
   tamed, lingering and contented.

Then our feet will as feet must, and dance.
   Yours gently upon mine to bear your matter;
and so, to measure the remainder of our time
   on land together before I,
still the sailor, ever the sailor, entrenched in sailorhood –
   hence mortal, quivering, adrift and doomed –
set once again
   to see you from a distance and to know
that beauty never tasted fairer
   smelt deviner, sounded purer, stuck more salient
in this, one sailor's core.

There are yet continents and poles untouched.
   But they will wait, and they will shift
their shelves for newer hands.
   You are my final find, my last discovery.
Should I, with you, no longer stay, but beg your leave to sea
   to set – to drift, to love and already to remember,
we two, we happy two, will rest for all posterity
   as conquering maiden, conquered man.

Aubade to Marit – Never Sung

I.

Now let us go to contemplate that hill
where flowers spit their seeds, intent to show
unbridled bits to daybreak's afterglow—
like tumblers hurled up at one boy's will
to make the skies grow dark; the rooftops, still.
A burst of liberated doves that know:
while boys stay stuck, *these* birds are free to go;
yet doves return to sip their pigeon's swill.
Night prods, commands her new moon to retire,
then drops a purled curtain as I think
of how we might promote dawn's primrose fire
to draw you gently out and to the brink
and there, with pink unfurled, probe your desire.
Yet you demur—and so, like doves, we sink.

II.

We have, like dolts reduced to abacus,
found too few days to let them pass in haste.
So, rather than remain demurely chaste,
let's find some ground and make it *ruinous!*
First, from the firmament enfolding us,
I'll snatch a string of stars to gird your waist.
Should jealous skies demand they be replaced,
we'll chuck *that* chore to cuckold Calculus!

But, in the meantime, once more to that hill –
to ride your string of stars as carousel
from dawn till dusk and only *there* to dare
to contemplate how we might then fulfill
our task if we have merely stars to tell
how passion makes of vanity a fair.

III.

Now close your eyes and ponder paradise:
how on that hill, sure-footed antelope
would take two lovers' hearts high up a slope
where one prim pout from Prudence might suffice
to gainsay quick elopement – *lust's* device –
and there, to show how Cupid's double scope
and steady aim at one small thing called hope,
would shoot to seal our vows not once, but twice!
And *then* we'd finally strip that robe that hides,
that chides your flesh to keep itself discreet,
remote, and from my own, quite separate –
while I, with dawn, which over hilltops rides,
would slip upon you like a silken sheet
and wrest that thermostat from 'Temperate!'

IV.

The sun—awake and stretching—mounts our hill
to prod his infant dawn to one quick pace
lest through equivocation, we lose place
and have to settle for some slacker's thrill.
So, let me ask what love will drive *you* still
when ice-bound nights and cutting winds give chase
to lovers' lyres and summer's last embrace
since with my thrust denied, I sense a chill?
Real love, you claim, works best by standing toe
to toe with neighbors over some dumb fence
as snow begins to melt and turn to mud.
While lust, you say, would in its frenzied flow
play far too fast—then lose its subtle sense
precisely when our love needs fuel to bud!

V.

Dawn hikes up on her heels, though barely born,
and sends her sullen glowworms home to bed
to sleep with gluttony, now slaked and fed.
Yet looking back, night casts a mother's scorn
upon this child of sun and lover-morn:
this *bastard* kid, who has with antics bled
fast fireflies of light and left instead
night bald, and of her stars, completely shorn—
until, that is, the sun notes your restraint
and sends the moon a remonstrating frown,

which she reflects with patient, lunar grace.
Both sun and moon first register complaint,
then from departing clouds take back their crown,
and, in the end, retrieve *their* rightful place.

A Year of Musing
Dangerously

January

Let's dim the lights, then flog the floor,
   and show our cherished guests the door
as we bid fond farewell to gay December.

Then *will* you take that holly down
   and help me deck these halls in brown
to bury whole whom we cannot dismember?

If next, our axe might broach the bin
   and strike upon some lode of gin,
can we then seal within this wretched season –

   and give ourselves (what better serves
the tra-la-la of tinseled nerves)
   a nightcap to the folly of our reason?

February

My cat walks in on foggy feet,
   and I light up like Frost.
She slurs a purr – like dykes in heat
   at face-off in Lacrosse.

With marbled eyes, she looks askance,
   as if to say 'How twee
that you should now romance a dance
   that *Sandburg* wrote for *me*' –

which then reminds me that her nails
   might profit from a clipper;
but as no sharper tool avails,
   I lay siege with a slipper

which, flung in haste, cannot erase
   my misplaced attribution.
And yet she's just a cat, I think,
   while I *dog execution...*

"You sound like Pound!" now lastly seems
   insipid with conviction –
as I know solecisms earn
   the Academy's eviction.

That Frost is more at ease with fog
   is hardly feline news,
since she views skewering similes
   as how *poor* poets lose.

And yet, if cats are what it takes
   to shake up my redaction,
just like the grave, I'll grind this knave
   with staves into retraction.

March

Last winter's mad-dog clutches
   made a mess of this spring spree,
then snatched away my crutches
   and dried up my do-re-mi.

Now, Lordie, if that's all ya gots
   of life on one short shelf,
I think I'll find some warmer spots
   on which to sun myself.

In truth, my kind don't give a damn
   about the world's widgets,
'cause living here, out on the lam,
   we can't connect the digits.

So if this godforsaken pit
   ain't nothing but a ruse,
allow me first to bitch a bit
   before I self-abuse.

It's true that what I wanted
   wasn't quite the thing I got,
since here I hit the skids galore
   as tongue-tied polyglot.

A shame, too, that I simply can't
   produce some better *skit*,
as that might put my Swedish rant
   to bed before I split

to babble with the best of 'em
   of *mierda, Scheiß', гавно* –
and then, conclude my stratagem
   with a brummagem 'no show.'

April

It's April again, with its wretched refrain
   of the taxman, who cometh a-calling.
Am I then to blame if I shudder in shame
   at his short-list to which we keep falling?

I don't doubt he's right – after all, there's tonight
   when with you I'd much rather be balling;
since like Mother Earth, we've some sense of the worth
   of what he and his Hubbard find galling.

And so, we restrain our critique of the rain
   as the reason we're both now recalling
that May days and flowers are grateful for showers
   that taxmen regard as appalling.

But try as he might to indict us tonight
   for sedition, perdition and stalling,
we both know this human just lacks the acumen
   to amortize amorous mauling.

May

If May weren't so smashing,
   I think I'd be cashing
my shoes in for life at the Cape –

whose fêtes I'd go crashing
   while probably bashing
my head in on fermented grape.

If May were less thrilling,
   no doubt Jeffrey Skilling
would leave us all dumbly agape;

but Lay's no less chilling
   and is likely shilling
for guys who think love envies rape.

If May weren't compelling,
   I might think of selling
Lay's version on videotape;

but nothing's propelling
   my urge to try telling
his sheep *de Panurge* to escape.

If May weren't compounding,
   their need to keep sounding
like dullards evading a scrape,

I might just try founding
   a trust that seeks grounding
in other than 'U. S. of Ape.'

June

If lights, at last, go dim in June
    on May's swift kick of luck,
will spry July plea out some goon
    to plunder August's pluck?

While crawling through my attic hall,
    I sense an end impendingas
creditors, in panicked call,
    assail my overspending

 on one young love whose brazen breach
    of trust turned out the light
just as the sea waved off the beach
    and bade us both goodnight –

which left me free to contemplate
    how rashly I could purge
those random memories that prate
    once hope abandons urge.

July

With summer in the groove,
   I finally move
to kiss the kids a
   rachety goodbye,

but pray our makeshift pawl
   called 'provenance'
will prove to outwit
   jaundice and July

to keep their sudden stall
   at 'sustenance'
remote and safe from
   one dread dragonfly

whose appetite would claim –
   at least restrain –
their Maine event: our
   swansong lullaby.

August

August is the month that always wins –
   except when it decidedly does not.

To wit:

when spring's proud vows succumb to wilt and rot
   as lady love eludes your gnarled knot;
or cabala and kids condense your plot –
   and you, in retribution, flush their pot;

then August's just another month that spins –
   perhaps because September spurns her spot.

September

Try not to remember how once in September
   I fought to keep both boats afloat,
as "friends" would all gather to lambaste our blather,
   then vote on who'd best cooked whose goat.

Instead, watch the children in early December
   when Christmas is still quite remote,
since kids know that dads' lack of facts in November
   might mean one less warm winter coat.

* * * * * * * * *

The heat's less oppressive, yet I'm still obsessive
   about my late lover – don't gloat.
Instead, let's bring Smirnov to bed for a burn-off,
   then swill with a swell anecdote:

while true that her aura (she's *no* Petrarch's Laura)
   may stick thick as thieves in my throat,
let's not forget Laura, too, once had an aura
   of crepuscule – now creosote.

October

If fall portends a final rest
   stop far from our late plummet,
let's dip into your wedding chest
   and grab a grommet from it

to rile the scam and halt our skid
   a plum's throw from the summit,
of where, from wiser eyes, we hid
   before we had to slum it

beneath the skirts of a brazen maid
   whose bawdiness once beckoned
to frenzied folks on lemonade
   now squeezing every second

out of a life that would parade
   as comfy self-reliance
while keeping up a poor charade
   of personal defiance.

November

Very little of November
   really grabs me in December
like my calendar, galumphing for the door.
   And yet nothing in my pocket
moves an angry inch to block it
   as I lock 'n' load, take aim, and strafe the floor.

Our new venture's sounding bleaker
   as I shake an eager beaker,
reprimanding one dumb barkeep to pour more –
   till, while *wrastling* a bottle,
I rip off its redneck throttle,
   and we shoot the shit as Buba sells the store.

       * * * * * * * * *

How deliciously seditious
   was our tedious little Prius
until nipping 'round the town lost all its lore.
   Then I found a hearse to hump it
with a samovar and strumpet
   who lit up my night like one bright Лада-whore.

So, let's sink this silly circus,
   write a book and pray that Kirkus
doesn't lead the sheep in bleating *Such a bore!* –
   since it's only daft December
whose last draft of "Kill the Sender"
   is how Kirkus geeks would render "Je t'adore."

December

Nothing born in late November
   – in this last gasp of the year –
feels so fragile in December
   as a smile before a tear.

Harvest moons may make me wonder
   why my once-too-livid Lear
railed like lightning seeking thunder,
   peaking, too, my frequent fear –

fear of what some might remember:
   as a sliced and diced career
into what this wry dissembler
   liked to call his 'favorite bier.'

What now bodes for next November
   if not Styx and one Bronx cheer?
Only Charon in December,
   striking out – and steering clear.

Lite Verse

A Low I. Q. Haiku

Two roads, in a 'hood,
   diverged. I hiked the high road –
and was justly mugged.

A Poet and a Gardener

A poet and a gardener,
   both spermatogenetic,
would bust a gut to bag a slut
   and call their *geste* frenetic.

And if a nymph in 'Net café
   goes yodeling on Yahoo,
she's daft to draft (to public) pix
   of her princessly ragoût.

'Cause not-so-bright cosmopolites,
   in too tight bathhouse pathos,
would slit a throat to mount her moat
   and drench the wench in bathos.

In potpourri delirium,
   where sage rues thyme in cruet,
they'd let rose marry marjoram
   and scatter catmint through it.

Yet if our nettled nymph avenged
   with sprigs of oleander,
I warrant oafs to Grecian urns
   – for sorrel – would unhand her.

But Mondays-through-Fridays Are Hellishly Long!

But Mondays-through-Fridays are hellishly long!
   occurs to me, lying in bed.
And yet, if a Sunday's religiously wrong,
   a Saturday stinks at the head.

So, what is the *one* day a guy can enjoy
   if not in his bed, in his head?
(I dare say a chick knows how best to annoy
   a guy seeking glory instead.)

And yet if I take this collection of days,
   subtracting the two that don't count,
I calculate little but work-a-day haze
   and chicks too reductive to mount.

It's all disconcerting and laughably cruel—
   this effort to rate and refine;
and so, I'll remain in this bed like a fool
   to pull on my pud and opine.

Caveat poeta: lectores mordent

Adults have little yen to read,
   and even less to deconstruct,
so let your work find wings to speed
   like water through an aqueduct.

Now if your piece behooves a chew,
   because odd parts feel clotted,
we're apt to think your retinue
   will opt for fuel less solid.

If riddled wit then gives the slip
   to bits still feeling fecal,
these may becloud your clever clip
   with dense and senseless treacle.

And if your lines lisp Derrida
   in stanzas too inflected,
our dodo crew, like dear Dada,
   may deem your verse affected.

So show some flair, Apollinaire,
   lest word-stews turn out fetid.
And take, for fuck's sake, proper care
   of expletives deleted!

As Browning meant, but didn't say
   of a ranter's anguished gasp:
your will to reach – feet stuck in clay –
   may just exceed your grasp.

Cold

A coxcomb cold, so I've been told,
   will mope around and natter,
then step right up and tap the glass
   whose mass it means to shatter.

But let's consider one small point
   as panes commence to clatter
like twittering birds atop tall trees –
   a class content to chatter

about some starlet's slow decline,
   as paparazzi scatter
to photograph a *younger* lass
   whose ass they'd rather flatter.

And if in jest, there is a gist –
   some pith to all my patter
re: photogs' uncouth cameras,
   it's this – *forget* the latter.

'Cause getting fat, or poor, or old –
   endemic to a ratter –
are time- and weather-tested means
   to expedite the matter.

Girl from Baku

I once idly wandered the wharfs of New York,
   carousing like Carroll, but hunting for sn*o*rk,
and saw there a girl set to pass on review:
   a petulant pet parvenue.

I curtailed my search on a quay in Par*ee*
   for a French lass *du jour* (but who'd *toujours* love me);
instead, vowed to wow this *"génue"* from Baku
   to love me till death us undo.

She sent me away – a degenerate jerk,
   to diddle with donkeys in dingy Dunkirk,
or else, to get clued in on ewes from Baku,
   who hoof it with didgeridoo.

And so from Москва, where I'd spied in a spa
   a spry thing from Riga in sporty red bra,
I sent the news home to my girl from Baku,
   who milked it like one mad emu.

I next found a floozie in boozie Berlin.
   "Just *try* her!" I hawked with the crux of a grin.
"De*lici*ously hip!" quipped my girl from Baku,
   who finger-licked lickerish Pooh.

I then stripped a kid of his id in Madrid,
   who'd offered me whores as baksheesh for my bid
to find him a strumpety girl from Baku,
   ignoring that I knew one, too.

I last hooked some kink in the heart of Helsink' –
   a pert pair who plied me with VSOPink.
I flung both Finns out for my girl from Baku…
   who finished me off with 'Fuck you!'

I Wish I Might've Found the Road to Oxbridge

(dedicated to Alfred Edward Housman)

I wish I might've found the road to Oxbridge,
   but lacking proper diction, I fell free;
instead, I found a way to roam to cleavage
   and felt my detour pay off handsomely.

It's 3 a.m., the Silent Hour

It's 3 a.m., the silent hour,
   without a hint of breeze;
and even mist won't move a flower
   unless to make it sneeze.

It's 3 a.m., a quiet time,
   when slugs seek slow romance
in enervating trails of slime
   that venerate their dance.

It's 3 a.m., and all is still,
   except for mother nature,
whose worms now work through moldered till
   to mine its nomenclature.

It's 3 a.m., and all is well,
   while Morpheus calls for sleep…
Hallo, what's this? Some kiss 'n' tell
   now priming me to peep?

It's *4* a.m.: the hour at which
   young love trades sweet for sour;
I think it best to bathe my itch
   in bubbles – or a shower.

June bug

June bug, is the rumor true
   about your soiled existence:
that, waiting for July to die,
   you toil in concupiscence?

I, myself, might chafe a bit
   if forced to love for grub.
But must you eat – you little shit –
   my only lonely shrub?

Saturn, in a neat retreat,
   devoured his brood with relish.
Ops dropped Jupiter on Crete
   once Saturn's mood turned hellish.

Myths are but an ancient means
   to say to lads and lasses:
dads eat genes, and bugs eat greens –
   so, cover *both* your asses.

Little Gets Riddled

Little gets riddled or ruddled or puddled
   that's not on tip-toes for a treat.
None of us can, when our senses get muddled,
   distinguish the tart from the sweet.

Just as the masses at Piggly Wiggly
   know that a tit's not a teat,
trying to rhyme with a word like 'molasses'
   is time better spent shooting skeet.

Some of our reason reacts to the rattle
   of brats who won't stay in their seat –
itching to snitch on the lowing of cattle
   while upchucking lunch at our feet.

Clearly, a poodle possesses a noodle,
   as poodles are partial to meat.
Felines, however, can sign with a doodle –
   thus mewing a pooch in defeat.

Done is this piece in just lickety-split, and so
   damn if it's still incomplete.
Not that these verses escape feeling rickety
   reeling out rhymes in retreat.

(Sometimes I think that a poet can blow it,
   if off by so much as a beat –
given that life is a trifle inchoate
   until it's a *fait accomplit!*)

Spring Bling – Ka-*ching!*

The whist of my wild wisteria
   is a game I wish I could play –
if only my wistful wisteria
   would willingly take me away.

The gist of my wistful wisteria
   is nothing I'd care to display;
I'd simply prefer less hysteria,
   and whispers of some better day.

            * * *

"How much wood would a dogwood dog
   if a dogwood could dog wood?"
"I think less wood than a *dog* would dog,
   and far less than a good dog should."

"Oh… then,

how much dog would a wood dog dog
   if a wood dog could dog dog?"
"He'd dog that dog as a wood dog would
   but my dog, thank God, ain't wood."

            * * *

My apple pines little for ocean;
   my apple pines still less for sea;
I opine my little green apple
   now pines for a pineapple tree.

* * *

If veronica's a viper
   and vibernum prefers camp
does that suggest verbena might
   then take it like a tramp?
.

      * * *

"You smell like syringa,"
   says beautiful Inge,
whose touch feels like sand to the sea.
   I get the bartender
to set his agenda
   on piña coladas for three.

"You bud like syringa,"
   says slightly drunk Inge
now lifting her skirt just for me,
   "and like my own finger
would lovingly linger
   bid you 'goodnight.'"

Acknowledgments

Paper publications:

"Turning Point in the Affairs of a Nation" in **The American Dissident**.
"Diminished Expectations" in **The Blind Man's Rainbow**.
"Not Enough" in **The Barbaric Yawp**.
"Uneasy Traders" in **The Lyric**.
"Flight 103 to Lockerbie: Happy Anniversary!" in **The Lyric**.
"Coitus" in **The International Journal of Erotica**.
"Aubade to Marit, Never Played" (blank verse version)in **The International Journal of Erotica**.
"Should I Miss Her Now in Winter?" **Wicked Hollow**.
"Flight 103 to Lockerbie: Happy Anniversary!" in **Aesthetica**.
"Epitaph: To My Children" and "I Rummage 'Round in My Safe Place" (the latter nominated for a Pushcart Prize) in **The Raintown Review**.
"Surrender," "Investment Counseling" and "Spell-unbounded" in **CritJournal**.
"The Silence of a Sunday" in **The Lyric**.
"Spell Unbounded" in **Tuesday; an Art Project**.
"So, *This* Is How Old Forests Feel" in **Grey Book Press**.
"A Tribute to the Humble Lilac" in **Trinacria**.
"It's Three a.m., the Silent Hour" and "If Love Is to Cartography What Romance Is to Maps" (the latter nominated for a Pushcart Prize in **Trinacria**.
"Aubade to Marit in C Minor" – a series of five sonnets, in **Trinacria**; also Sonnet V only in **Sonnetto Poesia**.
"February" and "I Prowl About My Garden" **The Feline Muse**.
"I Prowl About My Garden" in **Trinacria**.
"The Last Rose of Summer" in **Trinacria**.

"I Often Think I'd Like to Be" and "I Wish I Might've Found the Road to Oxbridge" in **Trinacria**.

My translation of Sergei Yesenin's "A Letter to My Mother" in **Trinacria**.

"There's Nothing Left but Cigarettes" in **Trinacria**.

"But Mondays-through-Fridays Are Hellishly Long," "Now, Where Would the First Wind Begin" and "A Body May with Wit Rebel" in **Trinacria**.

"Unherbed" (re-titled "Spell Unbounded," but published in this instance simply as "Unbounded") in **RATTLE**.

E-publications:

"Note to Walt Whitman" and "The Garden Lusts for Thrill Tonight" at **kenagain.freeservers**.

"Love in Winter Storage"; "To the Victor, All the Spoils"; "Sub Wisteria";"Deadheaded"; and "Diminished Expectations" at **ink-mag**.

"Investment Counseling" at **Quintessence encouraging great writing**

"Coitus" at **Erotica Readers & Writers Association. erotica-readers**.

"Waving Off the Last of Winter" at **Spillway Review**; then again at **ALongStoryShort**.

"Aubade to Marit, Never Played" (5 Petrarchan sonnets) at **EdificeWrecked**; then as "Aubade to Marit in C Minor" at **ALongStoryShort**; then at **Plum Biscuit**. The original blank verse version was published at **JustusRoux**. And lastly as "Aubade to Marit Haahr" at **TheLinnet'sWings**.

"Discreetly Jettisoned" at **GirlsWithInsurance**.

"Love Becomes You in the Fall" at **SalomeMagazine**.

"God Bless Amerika" at **MadHattersReview**.

"Warning to Minors: Adult Literature" and "Stratifying the Stress" at **ThievesJargon**.

"Busted" at **GirlsWithInsurance**.

"Uneasy Traders" and "Epitaph: To My Children" at **ALongStoryShort**.

"January"; "February"; "March"; "April"; *"Caveat Poeta: Lectores Mordent";* "Girl from Baku"; "Flight 103 to Lockebie: Happy Anniversary"; "Epitaph: To My Children"; "Should I Miss Her Now in Winter?"; "SAD Saps"; "The Real Object of Her Affections"; "Cold"; and "Narcissus' First Encounter with Echo at the Weeping Well" at **LauraHird.**
"Our Blackout" at **GirlsWithInsurance.**
"I Miss Her Most in Winter" and "Your Search" at **A Long Story Short**
"Deadheaded" and "Diminished Expectations" at **A Long Story Short.**
"9/11/03: to Debra P." at **OpiumMagazine.** "Coitus" and "Ode to a New Boss, and Brief" at **ZygoteInMyCoffee.**
"Love in Winter Storage," "Epilogue to a 'Splendid' Love Affair"; "Sub Wisteria"; "Deadheaded"; and "Diminished Expectations" at **SouthernHum.**
"9/11/03 (to Debra P.)" and "The Garden Lusts for Thrill Tonight" at **ALongStoryShort.**
"Recidivism" at **MindfireReview** and at **PWReview.**
"Family Planning" and "The Ethos of Capital-isthmus" at **PWReview.**
"Love Becomes You in the Fall" and "Narcissus Undone" at **ALongStoryShort.**
"A Poet and a Gardener" at **DifferentVoices**; at **ZygoteInMyCoffee**; and at **VoidMagazine.**
"Caned and Disabled" at **SouthernHum.**
"Screwered" at **VoidMagazine**; at **ALongStoryShort**; and at **3:AM.**
"Flight 103 to Lockerbie - Happy Anniversary!" "Should I Miss Her Now in Winter" and "Love in Winter Storage" at **ALongStoryShort.**
"I Remember When I Was a Player" at **ALittlePoetry.**
"To a Happier New Year" and "SAD Saps" at **ALongStoryShort.**
"Recidivism" at **thebreath.**
"Coitus" at **CentrifugalEye.**
"Cold" and "Blizzard" at **ALongStoryShort.**

"The Real Object of Her Affections" and "Surrender"
   at **ALongStoryShort**.
"Recidivism" and "Epilogue to a Splendid Love Affair"
   at **ALongStoryShort**.
"Our Blackout" and "Stratifying the Stress" at **ALongStoryShort**.
"Busted" and "I Like the Light of Summerscapes" at
   ALongStoryShort.
 "I Miss Her Most in Winter" at **SouthernHum**.
"Caveat Poeta: Lectores Mordent," at **ALongStoryShort**.
"Blizzard" at **3:AM**.
"Girl from Baku" at **3:AM**; at **Dogmatika**; at **Sliptongue**;
   and at **ISMs Press**.
"I Like the Orange, but *Love* the Black" and "Out of a
   Rock, *NOW!*" at **ALongStoryShort**.
"August," "September" and "A Body May with Wit Rebel"
   at **TheCentrifugalEye**.
"Family Planning" and "I Remember When I Was a Player"
   at **ALongStoryShort**.
"I Rummage 'Round in My Safe Place" at **ALongStoryShort**.
"January"; "February"; "March"; "April"; "May"; "June"; "July";
   "August"; "September"; "October"; and "November" first
      at **ALongStoryShort**; then at **DeadDrunkDublin**.
"February" at **HazardCat** and then at **TheFelineMuse**.
"Flight 103 to Lockerbie: Happy Anniversary!" and "Out of a
   Rock, *NOW!*" at **The Linnet's Wings**.
"December" at **DeadDrunkDublin**.
"Coitus" at **Sliptongue**.
"From Dust We Come, to Dust We Go" at **3rdActs**.
"A Rasher of Poems for Snarky Children" (including: "What
   Warmth Is There in One Old Tree"; "Hurly-Burly"; "Little
   Miss Muffet"; "Nolens Volens"; "This Rain That Wears No
   Raincoat"; "Habeas Corpus"; and "Four(teen)-letter Words")
      at **TheLinnet'sWings**.
"A Heart Is Not a Valentine" at **AscentAspirations**.
"The Ethos of Capital-isthmus" at **Chantarelle'sNotebook**
   and at **TheLinnet'sWings**.

"'Caned and Disabled" at **EvergreenReview**.

"Nolens Volens" at **ThePartyOfTheFirstPart**.

"June bug"; "So, This Is How Old Forests Feel"; and "I Watch a Spider Spin Her Web" at **Per Contra Spring 2009 Light Verse Supplement**.

"June bug"; "From Dust We Come – to Dust We Go"; and "There's Nothing Left but Cigarettes" at **TheNewFormalist**.

The last stanza only of "They Say that 'Orange' Has No Pair" at **Dogzplot**.

"The Ethos of Capital-isthmus"; "Any Dope Can Write a Ditty" (one stanza only); "Patriot Act"; and "Ode to a New Boss, and Brief" at **Clockwise Cat**.

"So,*This* Is How Old Forests Feel" at **TheCentrifugalEye**.

"Screwvenir" at **Litsnack**.

"Qui Tacet, Consentit" at **Lucid Rhythms**.

"It's Spring – Ka-*ching!"* at **ABCTales**.

"Spell Unbounded"; "Uneasy Traders"; *"Caveat Poeta: Lectores Mordent"*; "Stratifying the Stress"; and "May" at **theHyperTexts**.

My translation of Sergei Yesenin's poem "A Letter to My Mother" at **Elimae**; at **theHyperTexts**; and finally at **TheLinnet'sWings**.

"The Last Rose of Summer" and "There's Nothing Left but Cigarettes" at **TheLinnet'sWings**.

About the Author

Russell's work (prose, poetry and photography) has been widely published in print and on the WorldWideWeb. His first novel, ***Trompe-l'oeil,*** appeared at both Amazon-Kindle and Smashwords in March of 2011, as did his two collections of short stories and one novella (one in each): ***Stories in the Key of C. Minor.*** and ***The Dead Don't Bitch.***

His memoir, ***Girl from Baku***—previously published by ISMs Press on the 'Net—also appeared at both Amazon and Smashwords in 3/11.

This is his first, only and last publication of poetry in book form.

He believes, with Hobbes, that "life is short, brutish and nasty." He also believes, with Donne, however, that art is long; and that no man is one, entire of itself—either an island or a work of art.

www.ingramcontent.com/pod-product-compliance
Lightning Source LLC
Chambersburg PA
CBHW070457100426
42743CB00010B/1662